YOUR KNOWLEDGE HAS VALUE

Bibliographic information published by the German National Library:

The German National Library lists this publication in the National Bibliography; detailed bibliographic data are available on the Internet at http://dnb.dnb.de .

Imprint:

Copyright © 2018 GRIN Verlag
Print and binding: Books on Demand GmbH, Norderstedt Germany
ISBN: 9783346025777

This book at GRIN:

https://www.grin.com/document/497484

Rashida Thielhorn

The Imagery of Nature in Derek Walcott's Poetry

GRIN Verlag

GRIN - Your knowledge has value

Since its foundation in 1998, GRIN has specialized in publishing academic texts by students, college teachers and other academics as e-book and printed book. The website www.grin.com is an ideal platform for presenting term papers, final papers, scientific essays, dissertations and specialist books.

Visit us on the internet:

http://www.grin.com/

http://www.facebook.com/grincom

http://www.twitter.com/grin_com

Johann Wolfgang Goethe-Universität
Sommersemester 2018

American Studies

Poetry from Somewhere Else: Derek
Walcott, Seamus Heaney, Joseph Brodsky

The Imagery of Nature in Derek Walcott's Poetry

Abgabetermin: 14.09.2018

Rashida Thielhorn

American Studies/Romanistik BA

8. Fachsemester

List of Contents

I. Introduction

I.1.About the Poet and his Writings

Sir Derek Alton Walcott, who was often referred to as Derek Walcott (he also signed with this form), was born in 1930 in Castries, St. Lucia and died at his home in Cap Estate, St. Lucia in 2017.

Walcott was a well-known Caribbean poet, playwright and painter who also received the Nobel Prize for literature in 1992 among other literary prizes and nominations such as an Obie Award (1971, for his play "Dream on Monkey Montain"), a MacArthour Foundation "genius award", a Royal Society of Literature Award, the Queen's medal for peotry, the inaugural OCM Bocas Prize for Caribbean Literature, the 2011 T. S. Elliot Prize for his book of Poetry *White Egrets* and the Griffin Trust for Excellence in Poetry Lifetime Recognition Award in 2015.

He also had teaching positions at Boston, Columbia, Rutgers and Yale and both of his grandmothers were said to have been descended from slaves and "his decision to write mostly in standard English brought attacks from the Black Power movement in the 1970s." (Lea)

McDonald Dixon, Walcott's longtime friend and even St. Lucian author himself declared in an 2003 telephone interview:

"While his friends played the boyish games of cowboys and crooks,
Derek's sense for excitement was filled by exploring literature that

1

graced his hands. It was this thirst that unraveled the inner voice

which he would use as a catalyst for his self-expression." (Telephone

Interview 2003) (Hosier,3).

Throughout his career he received many literary awards, often for his epic poem collections, taught and served as a professor at different universities such as the University of Alberta (Canada) and the University of Essex (England) or the Boston University and occasionally painted excellent art works with water colors during his free time. Derek Walcott's father, Warwick Walcott, who died when the poet and his twin brother were not more than one year old, may have passed on some of his talent to his son: The artifacts he bequeathed to his family were books and paintings. The loss of the father at such an early age and his missing while growing up and developing to a young matured man is mirrored in many of Walcott's literary works.

Walcott's mother, Alix Maarlin Walcott, who was a teacher and run a school, enabled her son to publish his first collection of poems by paying a fee to send the script to Trinidad (just a few years after he had published his first single and religious poem at age 14 in a newspaper) at age 19 (the main topics were "the Caribbean, its history, scars of colonialism; language, power and place"). Many literary experts mention his Homeric epic poem *Omeros (1990)* as his best-known work and greatest achievement: "*Omeros* reimagines the Trojan War as a Caribbean fishermen's fight". (Magdalena De Gasperi) Derek Walcott also had a twin brother, the St Lucian playwright, screenwriter, painter, theater director, costume and set designer, lyricist and literary editor Roderick Walcott, and a sister called Pamela Walcott. In 1953, after graduation, Walcott moved to Trinidad and became a critic, teacher and journalist.

When reading Walcott's poetry or on closer examination of his paintings one can identify that there are symbols and metaphors that are often repeated in his works: naturalistic phenomena, such as different plants and their botanical and scientific correct names or the deep blue sea and sky and other symbols of nature. In his poems Sir Derek Alton Walcott used the imagery of nature to connect to his Caribbean heritage, to describe his own problems and experiences during child- and adulthood, and to emphasize the facets of traveling.

I.2.Walcott's Identity Crisis and the resulting Hybridity within his Poetry

Generally and broadly spoken Walcott's unique talent for the arts must have been more than "genetic gift" which he received from his deceased father. Walcott drew and developed his initial inspiration for writing poetry from living within the beautiful environment of the Caribbean island and St. Lucia. He was a highly gifted and multi-talented man who owned an outstanding eye for detail and artistic symmetry, also when creating the contrasts in his arts. In an 1971 interview Walcott recognized his own dual heritage with the following words:

I.3."The problem is to recognize African origins but not to romanticize them."

Further on he described himself with the following "poetic" words:

"I'm just a red nigger who love the sea,

I had a sound colonial education,

I have Dutch, nigger and English in me,

And either I'm nobody, or I'm a nation."

(Walcott; Morhan, p.1)

Despite the fact that Walcott, regarding his own word, was always "divided by the veins" since he did not only originate from English and African ancestry, but also used to live at the *French*-speaking part of the Caribbean island. Walcott called his own writing a "mulatto style" and "wished the multiracial, polyglot islanders to liberate themselves and really celebrate their hybrid culture that actually represents all the world's major cultures." (Morhan, p.2)

According to Morhan Walcott also "wished for a future where the dilemma of being black in skin and being white in mind can be solved irrevocably."

In an interview with David Montenegro Derek Walcott also described how he himself and many other authors and writers are "prisoners":

Walcott demonstrates how "narrowed" many modern poets are: in the end he even compares the poets, including himself, to prisoners: they often have a jail inside and are judges and prisoners at the same time. (p.87): " [...] I would say that every poet is imprisoned in a system that is himself, that he is jailed in himself, and that effort to get out of that jail is is the struggle he has or the defiance he has in having the guts to use the next word without the safety or the cliché of repetition. [...] The inner prison that exists is one that's outside and yet is inside the totalitarian regime".

II. Comparing two Poems and their Naturalistic Motifs

II.1. Derek Walcott's "Collected Poems 1948-1984":

From Sea Grapes: *Sea Grapes*

In 1976 Derek Walcott wrote the poem *Sea Grapes*, which is also part of his collection "Collected Poems (1948-1984) and part of the poem collection "From Sea Grapes" within the book: the title itself provides the reader an ambiguity (double meaning): On the one hand sea grapes are a type of a green algae, which is also known as "green caviar" and green caviar is traditionally used at the Philippines for preparing dishes.

On the other hand sea grapes refer to a specific type of grapes, green in color and bitter and sour in taste. The grapes grow typically in the Caribbean coastal area, are known for their unique taste and are poisonous, when still unripe . When perfectly ripened, the sea grapes are used for some special dishes too: In Caribbean cooking the typical sea grapes are used for making jelly, salsa as a side to certain dishes, salads, Focaccia and other delicious meals.

The poet from Caribbean heritage does not only refer to fruits or an algae, but used the sea grapes as a metaphor and an allegory, emphasizing the bitterness of making decisions. The poem describes the conflict between obsession and taking responsibility; an inner conflict which many people carry and have to solve personally. Both problems are directly mentioned in the poem. Like other works of Walcott (for example famous "Omeros", which is an adaption to Greek Homer's Odyssey) "Sea Grapes" counts to the epic and heroic poetry: it is a dactylic hexameter consisting of six stanzas and also connects to ancient Greek mythology. The main character is the famous Greek's mythology's hero Odysseus, who after he won the Trojan war (see also "Omeros) is confronted with many obstacles and seeks to finally return home, to his family, his wife and his son.

His greatest inner conflict is that despite the fact that he is deeply longing for his family, he is also often confronted by temptations, which he personally finds hard to resist: for example the beautiful woman on the islands, who he met during his long journey. Odysseus afterwards finds himself in the dilemma of resisting the obsession caused by the beautiful woman and taking responsibility for his own family. As a husband and father he finally makes the right decision and chooses to return home.

6

Walcott used the sour Sea Grapes as a metaphor for obsession: the protagonist is captured by his feelings; between guilt and dishonesty and it feels bitter (like the taste of unripe, poisonous sea grapes) to him to choose responsibility over obsession and being plagued by his conscience. In the third stanza the poet even mentions the (sea) grapes: "[...] longing, under gnarled sour grapes, is like the adulterer hearing Nausicaa's name in every gull's outcry." (Walcott, 297). Nausicaa is in Greek mythology and Homer's "Odyssey" the daughter of the King and Queen of Phaeacia and in the myth she saves shipwrecked Odysseys and they fall in love, but do not marry. Nausicaa can be seen here as the direct antagonist towards Odyssey's wife and also as the reason why the grapes are "gnarled", like a love that has been faded before it even really started. In the end of the poem Walcott concludes that "The classics can console. But not enough" (Walcott, 297), which could be a hint that for him this kind of dilemma never really disappeared and is still unsolved in modern times.

In the poem collection "From Sea Grapes [1976]" there are also other poems, which refer to the poet's home St. Lucia ("Sainte Lucie", Walcott, p.309), Greek mythology, biblical stories ("Adam's song", Walcott, p. 302) and even sour fruits ("Sunday Lemons", Walcott, p.298). The poem English-French "Sainte Lucie" does not only refer to Walcott's heritage and home, but consists of passages, which earlier used to be components of "Sea Grapes".

II.2. Derek Walcott's "Collected Poems 1948-1984": From Midsummer: *XIV*

The poem "XIV/*With the frenzy of an sold snake shedding its skin*" (Walcott, p. 476) consists of 21 lines, only one stanza and the rhyme scheme abcadefdghiijkljmkmj.

The poem was written in 1984, has the length of one page and is part of the poem collection "From Midsummer", which is also included in "Derek Walcott – Collected Poems 1948-1984".

In the beginning of the poem Walcott compares the speckled, twisted and worn road to the forest with a "skin-shedding snake", which crawls its way into nature. The shedding snake could be seen as a metaphor or even as a biblical symbol, which Walcott often used in his writings: The fact that the reptile is shedding depicts how something old and past transforms into something newer, only by itself. It is a prediction how a childhood memory develops to Walcott's later role in adulthood. In the bible the snake is also an important symbol for immortality and the (passing) time itself.

Like before in "Sea Grapes" Walcott here also remembers a typical Caribbean product of nature: the "Dasheen leaves", also known as "Taro leaves" or "Elephant Ears" are leaf/root vegetables, which are believed to be one of the earliest cultivated plants and already described by the famous Swedish botanist, physician and and zoologist Carl Linnaeus. They are the leaves of the tropical American plant

Colocasia Esculenta and are used mainly in Southern Caribbean cooking, for example for the spinach-like Caribbean dish "Callaloo".

The poem recalls a childhood memory of Derek Walcott: he and his twin brother Roderick Walcott (in the poem only "the twins" are directly mentioned) visit an elderly lady, called Sidone, listen to her stories and are "mesmerized".

After reading "Nobody's Nation: Reading Derek Walcott" by Paul Breslin, the readership is able to conclude that Sidone was the great-aunt of the two twin-brothers and she used to tell them uncountable folk-lore stories, which still inspired Derek's writings in modern times:

> "Middle-class St. Lucians sometimes regarded local folk-lore
>
> and folk traditions as embarrassing crudities to be left behind,
>
> but this was not so in Walcott's family. His great-aunt, *Sidone*
>
> Wardrope, would recite folk tales for the two brothers when
>
> they visited her in the country; Harold Simmons, who taught
>
> Walcott and St. Omer painting, was also a folklorist, one of the
>
> first educated St. Lucians to take the island's vernacular culture
>
> as worthy of serious study."
>
> (Breslin, p.13)

In the end of the short poem indicates how this elderly madam inspired him to write and may be one of the main reasons why he became a respected writer and poet: "In the gully of her voice shadows stood up and walked, her voice travels my shelves". The shelves could thereby be filled with Walcott's writings and as well with books he was inspired to read.

Another naturalistic symbol in the poem is the mimosa, called "Ti-Marie". "Ti-Marie" on the one hand refers to a later-written book of the same title, written in 1988 by Valerie Belgrave (a historic but fiction book about 18th-century Trinidad and a forbidden love-story between a black heroine and a white hero) and to Trinidad's shame plant, *Mimosa Pudica,* a sensitive plant which is also known as "Touch-me-not, Sensitive Grass, Shame Bush, Shame Face, Shame Lady, Shame Weed, common sensitive-plant, shameplant, TickleMe Plant, Shy plant, Sleeping grass and Prayer Plant" (healthbenefits.com). The „shy" plant is said to have positive and health-benefitial effects such as curing insomnia, arthritis, asthma, diabetes, high blood-pressure and other chronic diseases.

The blossoms, roots, leaves and even the seeds of the Mimosa plant are therefore used to produce the "medicine" for treatments of different sicknesses: The leaves are the dried to mix a special paste, which can for example be applied on the skin. Meanwhile the seeds of the plants are also dried an then grind like spices for cooking, to create a specific powder with healing abilities.

III. Walcott as a painter and the "Facets of Traveling"

Painting as a form of art was taught to Derek Walcott by Harold Simmons, who was a mentor to him and the designer of the St. Lucian flag. In 2007, Walcott's water color paintings were also exhibited in New York City at the Anita Shapolsky Gallery, along with the art of other writers. The exhibition was called: "The Writer's Brush: Paintings and Drawing by Writers".

Later his colorful watercolor paintings, which are also collected in his works "Tiepolo's Hound" or "Another Life", often depict colored people including himself for example in the act of painting itself, the Caribbean coasts, cliffs and the sea of St. Lucia and other places and other typical Caribbean motifs of nature. (See artnet.com, junekellygallery.com, etc.).

The naturalistic motifs which seemed to be a source of endless inspiration to the famous poet and Nobel laureate, also often occurred in his typical paintings: Walcott often managed to invite his beholders to share his intimacy as a painter and also his unique perception of the world and its surroundings.

Walcott can also be renamed as "the poet of the sea": not only did his poems often relate to the sea, but he is an islander himself (inhabitant of St. Lucia, which is placed on the small volcanic island nation Saint Vincent) and his sign was symbolizing water, meaning that he was born under the zodiac sign of Aquarius (born on 23th of January).

The poet himself was like the sea because "[...] the sea carries things between continents and casts them arbitrarily into new worlds. Its tides wash beaches and make them new as if continually starting again. It suggests power, even when calm, a Caribbean cool. It smooths, shapes, and transforms anything that comes into it, even rubbish. It is the sea as medium, then, a medium like art in its capacity to transform, that supplies Walcott with an endless metaphor. [...]"(T.J. Cribb, p.177)

"In a 1990 interview with J.P. White, Walcott, using the sea as a symbol for a way of movement and being that contrasts with those of what is conventionally called history, said: "With the sea, you can travel the horizon in any direction, you can go from left to right or from right to left. It doesn't proceed from A to B to C to D and so on.""(Taylor)

Concluding Cribb's quote one can assume that Sir Derek Walcott more than many other poets of the world represents the sea and traveling, because he has a divided heritage, having been European and Caribbean at the same time and he loved his heritage, even when it was hard to him to identify as the one or another; and especially he divided his lifetime, having lived in different continents. Also he liked to transport cultures over the ocean through his literary works and their different contents. The ocean also used to be one of his favorite painting motifs, because he often passionately portrayed the Caribbean coasts which he always used to know. The sea, the ocean and also many natural symbols like different plants and their correct botanical names have truly been Walcott's sources of endless inspiration; his inner muse and passionate drive.

IV. Conlusion

March 17th , 2017 marked the day in present history when the internationally well-known author Derek Walcott died at the age of 87 in Saint Lucia, his birthplace. The Guardian amongst other great American newspaper reported about the death of the Noble laureate, poet and playwright: Walcott was the poet "who moulded the language and forms of the western canon to his own purposes for more than half a century." (Lea) His poetry furthermore gained him an international reputation and the Noble Prize for literature in 1992,he was inspired by William Shakespeare and other famous poets; and he was also a very successful playwright, who wrote more than 80 plays which often discuss the problem of his Caribbean identity.

The former poet laureate Andrew Motion stated that Walcott was a "wise and generous and brilliant man" whose "rich sensualities of his writing are deeply evocative and also definitive, and its extraordinary historical and literary reach – in his long Homeric poem Omeros especially – gives everything in the present of his work the largest possible resonance. He will be remembered as a laureate of his particular world, who was also a laureate of the world in general." (Motion/Lea)

Beyond all the extraordinary achievements Walcott had during his lifetime, there was also a darker side to him: not only did he have identity troubles, but the years he spent as a teaching literature professor at different universities and his "teaching style" brought him into trouble: In the 1990s Walcott was accused for sexual harassment by two of his female students of two different universities. Afterwards he was also forced to withdraw his candidacy for the post of Oxford professor of poetry in the 2009 election.

Regrading Walcott's identity issues Taylor quotes – Pat Ismond, "Derek Walcott's Nobel Works", Caribbean Beat,Spring 1993 – in the following words:

"Accepting the legacy of the English language was to remain a

focal commitment for Walcott: but it came with the conflicting

problem of identity. How to fight free of the world of the colonizer

which is preserved in that legacy? The problem penetrated to a

deeper issue: the void of the region's absurd past, its condition

of historylessness. For Walcott, though, this historylessness

carried with it a pressing imperative: invention and new creation.

Quite earlyon, he settled upon the Crusoe-castaway figure as

the classic metaphor for the Caribbean's past and the ne-

cessity of creating a new. The figure Robinson Crusoe

embodies the isolation and abandonment of the Carib-

bean's uprooted peoples, and the corresponding

imperatives of survival."

Despite the fact that Derek Walcott seemed to have had trouble because of sexual harassment in more than one particular case, he was poet one has to know: In my personal opinion Walcott was a world-poet one has to know if working or studying within the field of literature or the science of languages. Even today Walcott and his work can still be seen as a milestone in English, Caribbean and especially world literature.

Furthermore Walcott will always remain an important example when in the omnipresent discussion of racism, slavery and identity because he proved the fact that people do not have to identify as "just" either black or white, because a single person can unite many heritages and different cultures within themselves. Identity can be defined as a complex structure: it is therefore more than just ancestry and what our DNA tells us; it is also more a feeling of belonging, the roots, a passion for culture and language, daily behavior and habits, and especially the way of living in general. One must not identify with one single heritage only, since all human beings have descendants and ancestors of different origins and cultures and therefore humanity is a multicultural creature in itself.

15

Works Cited

"Anita Shapolsky Gallery, 152 East 65th Street, NYC | Past Exhibits."
Anita Shapolsky Gallery 152   East 65th Street NYC,
anitashapolskygallery.com/newsite/25-2/.

Breslin, Paul. *Nobodys Nation: Reading Derek Walcott*. The University of Chicago
Press, 2001. Google Books

Britannica, The Editors of Encyclopaedia. "Taro." *Encyclopædia Britannica*,
Encyclopædia Britannica, Inc., 11 Oct. 2013, www.britannica.com/plant/taro-
plant.

Cribb, T. J. "'Walcott, Poet and Painter.'" *JSTOR*, www.jstor.org/.

Frey-Anthes, Henrik. "Schlange." *Startseite*, 1 June 2008,
www.bibelwissenschaft.de/wibilex/das-
bibellexikon/lexikon/sachwort/anzeigen/details/schlange-
1/ch/3657eaf67825283045375cc7f9b24dc9/#h1.

Gasperi, Magdalena De. "Derek Walcott." 2018 Power Point).

Gasperi, Magdalena De. *Poetry from Somewhere Else: Derek Walcott, Seamus
Heaney, Joseph Brodsky*. Johann Wolfgang Von Goethe Universität/Frankfurt Am
Main, 2018.

Hosier, Anna-Lee. "Walcott's Paintings, Poetry and Plays as Refelctions of the
Caribbean Landscape." *JSTOR*, www.jstor.org/.

Lea, Richard. "Nobel Laureate, Poet and Playwright Derek Walcott Dead, Aged
87." *The Guardian*, Guardian News and Media, 17 Mar. 2017,
www.theguardian.com/books/2017/mar/17/nobel-laureate-poet-and-playwright-derek-
walcott-dead-aged-87.

Lee, Sophia. "'Sea Grapes' Poem Analysis." *SoPhla*, 19 June 2011,
sophialee122.wordpress.com/2011/06/19/sea-grapes-poem-analysis/.

"Sea Grapes." *Encyclopædia Britannica*, Encyclopædia Britannica, Inc.,
www.britannica.com/topic/Sea-Grapes.

S. Mohan, "Treatment of Hybridity in the Poetry of Derek Walcott", International
Journal of Interdisciplinary Research in Arts and Humanities, Volume 2, Issue 1,
Page Number 17-18, 2017

Sylvia. "16 Health Benefits of Sensitive Plant (Touch Me Not)." *Health Benefits*, Health Benefits, 14 Sept. 2017, www.healthbenefitstimes.com/sensitive-plant/.

Taylor, Caroline. "Remembering Derek Walcott." *MEP Publishers | Trinidad & Tobago | Caribbean*, MEP Publishers | Trinidad & Tobago | Caribbean, 17 Mar. 2017, www.meppublishers.com/remembering-derek-walcott/#axzz5QQw7FNun.

Thieme, John. "" The Art of Seeing " : Painting and Metaphor in Derek Walcott's Poetry." *Academia.edu*, www.academia.edu/33244310/_The_Art_of_Seeing_Painting_and_Metaphor_in_Der ek_Walcotts_Poetry.

Walcott, Derek. „Sea Grapes"., „XIV". *Collected Poems, 1948-1984*. Noonday, 1994.

YOUR KNOWLEDGE HAS VALUE